Measuring

by Kathy I

Table of Contents

What Is Length?

How can you tell how long your room is? How can you tell how tall you are?

You can tell these things by measuring them. When you measure these things, you are measuring length. Length is the amount of space between two points.

They are measuring the length of the classroom wall. ▼

4 feet

The amount of space between the bottom of your feet and the top of your head tells the length of your body.

People measure length all the time.
They measure length when they
make clothes. They measure length
to find out how far apart places are.

500 feet

175 feet

▲ The amount of space between the barn and the house measures 175 feet. The barn and the horse stable are 500 feet apart.

How Did People Measure Length Long Ago?

People long ago measured length with parts of their bodies. Sometimes they measured length with their hands or feet.

Spread your fingers as far as you can. The length from your thumb to your little finger was called a span. The length of your foot was called a foot.

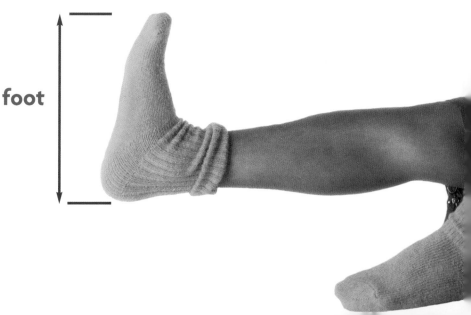

foot

span

What if you measured the length
of a playground with your foot?
What if an adult measured
the length with his foot?

Would you both get the same length? No!

People's bodies are different sizes.
One person's foot can be longer than
another person's foot. One person's span
can be longer than another person's span.

The man measures the playground to be 40 feet
when he measures with his own feet. ▼

When measuring with parts of the body, different people can come up with different lengths for the same thing!

The boy measures the playground to be 60 feet because his feet are much smaller than the man's. ▼

How Do People Measure Length Today?

To make measuring easier, people set up standard lengths. A standard length is the same everywhere in the world.

By using standard lengths, different people can measure the same thing and come up with the same length.

◀ Many people work together to build a house. They all need to measure in the same way.

Some standard lengths that people use are the inch, the foot, and the yard.

▲ This man measures the wood in feet and inches.

Other standard lengths that people use are the centimeter and the meter.

▲ This boy is measuring the bookcase with a meterstick. A meterstick measures centimeters and meters.

Today, people around the world
use standard lengths to measure things.